We hope this book about different families will lead children
and their parents to engage in conversation about their families.

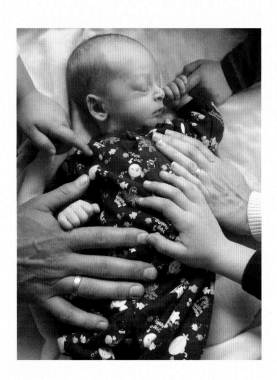

To Shelley Rotner and Hans Teensma, whose visual gifts
and hours of work made this book happen. — s.m.k.

To Sheila Kelly and Hans Teensma, whose insight
and integrity made this book come together. — s.r.

Families

by Shelley Rotner and Sheila M. Kelly

photographs by Shelley Rotner

holiday house/NEW YORK

There are
all kinds
of families.

Some families are $\textbf{big}$ and have

cousins, aunts, uncles, grandparents, and even **great-grandparents.**

Some are
small.

Sometimes the people in

a family look alike.

Sometimes they don't.

Some families have children born to them.

Some adopt.

Some children have
one parent.

Some have two —
a **mom** and a **dad**,

or two moms
or two dads.

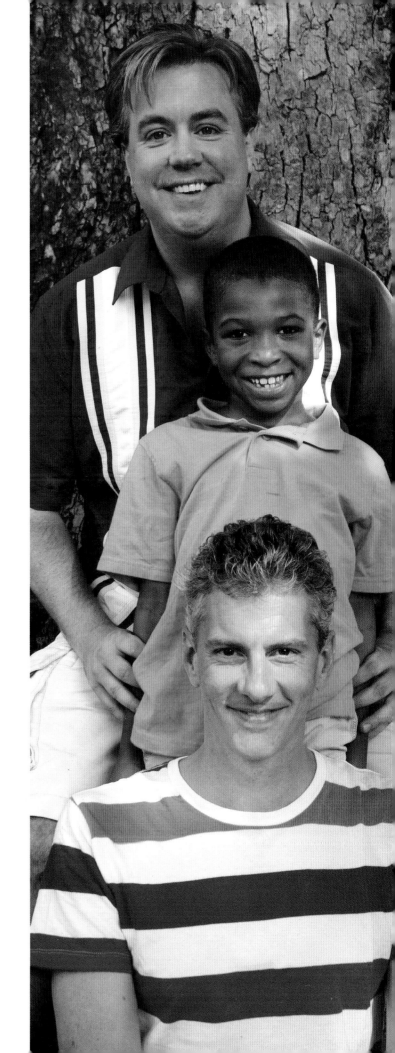

Others have a **grandparent**, an aunt, or an uncle living with them.

The people in a family
may not all live in the same place.

When members of a family live **far away,** they like to visit.

They get together
at celebrations and reunions.

Families have fun...

...being together.

They **help** one
another.

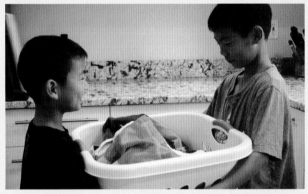

People in a family love

and care about each other.

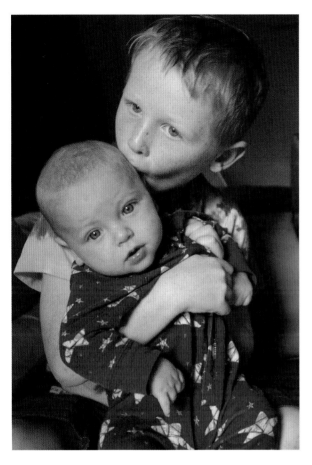

There are many **different** kinds of families.

What about yours?

Recently, research psychologists have found that children who developed
a strong family narrative from speaking with their parents about family
history and hearing family stories, both good and bad, exhibited greater
self-esteem and a feeling of control over their lives.

— S.M.K.

Text copyright © 2015 by Sheila M. Kelly and Shelley Rotner
Photographs copyright © 2015 by Shelley Rotner
All rights reserved.
HOLIDAY HOUSE is registered in the U.S. Patent and Trademark Office.
Printed and Bound in October 2014 at Toppan Leefung, DongGuan City, China.
www.holidayhouse.com
First Edition
1 3 5 7 9 10 8 6 4 2

Library of Congress Cataloging-in-Publication Data
Rotner, Shelley.
Families / by Shelley Rotner and Sheila M. Kelly ; photographs by Shelley Rotner. — First edition.
pages cm
Audience: Grades K to 3.
ISBN 978-0-8234-3053-6 (hardcover)
1. Families—Juvenile literature. I. Kelly, Sheila M. II. Title.
HQ744.R68 2015
306.85—dc23
2013032957